Quest For Truth

A TRUE STORY OF ONE MAN'S SEARCH FOR THE CHURCH THAT JESUS BUILT

By Tommie Lee Washington III

Special thanks to Greg Sprowl, for his love of the truth, and willingness to share it with a friend.

All scripture references use the New King James Version (NKJV)

© Copyright 2010 Tommie Lee Washington   All Rights Reserved
TOMMIELEEWASHINGTON.COM

Saint Mary's

Total darkness slowly turned to light as the smell of bacon sizzling in a rod iron pan told my senses that there was a breakfast being orchestrated in the kitchen. It was a breakfast like that which only my father's culinary artistry could manifest. The smell of scrambled eggs, bacon, toast, and grits were a carnival for my nose, causing my eyes to pop wide open and my body to leap out of my bunk bed, most likely waking my brother as he slept on the bottom bunk below me. As I quickly made my way, salivating toward the kitchen, my assumption was realized. Dad was at his usual Saturday morning ritual, creating a breakfast as only a Chief Warrant Officer could.

"Good Morning Troop! Are you ready for some grub?" he asked. I responded in blissful adoration, "Yes, please!" As soon as he set that plate full of southern hospitality down in front of me, it was on like Donkey Kong. I tore into that breakfast like there was no tomorrow. Dad was the only one who would make a big breakfast like this, and he only had time to do it on Saturdays. So Saturday mornings were always a special occasion that I looked forward to.

I guess Dad could have made the breakfast on Sundays as well, but on most Sunday mornings, for several years when I was around eight years old, Mom and Dad would send my siblings and I to church. My mother was a very classy lady who always wanted her children to look their best and be well mannered. So Mom always made sure we were all neatly dressed in our "Sunday Best" while we waited for our ride from our next-door neighbor.

When all the kids were ready, we would sit in the living room and wait until we heard "Honk Honk!" It was "Reverend Venerable," the minister of Saint Mary's Methodist Church in Burlington City, New Jersey, letting us know that he was ready to take us to church. Since he lived right next door to us, he offered to give my siblings and I a ride to Saint Mary's on Sunday mornings. I'm sure my parents saw that as a prime opportunity to have some peace and quiet for a couple hours. They also wanted us to get a religious education, so they let us go. Both of my parents were believers in God and Jesus as His Son. And on occasion, they would come with us to worship, but usually only on Holidays or special days like Mother's Day.

Sometimes when I was outside playing in the yard, I'd see the "Reverend" and we would talk. The conversations never lasted too long though. I guess as an eight-year-old, I was more interested in riding my bike than talking about church stuff. We didn't attend Saint Mary's every Sunday, but I can remember going there quite often. My most memorable experience at that church was when they announced their Vacation Bible School during the summer. At that time in my life I was very shy. The thought of going to VBS had me terrified. I didn't mind going to Saint Mary's occasionally with my siblings. But to be left there alone – no way! My Dad had to practically drag me there. In hindsight, I think he was encouraging me to go in order to help me overcome my shyness.

When I got there I was my usual, very shy, self. The teacher was cordial when I was introduced to her, but the sound of my heart beating like a kettle drum was so pronounced, I didn't hear a word she said. The VBS was held in an old building that was not connected to the normal church building that I was accustomed to worshipping in. Sitting before me was a group of children and church workers that, at the time, seemed like monsters waiting for my Dad to leave so they could devour me.

After minutes of unsuccessful negotiations with my father about not staying, I finally gave in and had a seat. First, we started with some songs I was familiar with. Then, we made a craft with construction paper, paint and glue. After that, we heard a Bible story from one of the teachers, then took a break and had sandwiches, chips, and Kool-Aid for lunch. Before I knew it, I was warming up to the whole situation. Much to my surprise, by the end of the day I had so much fun that I didn't want to leave. Needless to say, that Vacation Bible School day left a real positive impression on me that I still remember vividly to this day. What I didn't realize at the time was that it was a huge step forward on the path of my spiritual journey.

<u>Germany</u>

My father was in the Army and that meant that I was an "Army Brat." Or at least that's what they called children of those serving in the Army. I was nine years old when we left New Jersey and moved to Stuttgart, Germany, the country my mother was from. People called my siblings and I "mixed" because my mother was German and my father was African American, but on the Army base that wasn't a big deal. Lots of kids were "mixed". I had friends who were white, black, Philipino, Japanese, you name it. It was a melting pot of different cultures that I found to be an exciting and hilarious experience. I say "hilarious" because all my friends had the same sense of humor that I had. That's probably what brought us together. I'll never forget TJ and Reggie when I was in 7th grade, living in Geissen Germany. We kept each other laughing so much, I actually got an award for perfect attendance that year because I loved going to school. Not because of my teachers, mind you, but because TJ and Reggie were there. Now don't get me wrong, I still did all of my work and actually got pretty good grades.

Of course, I was too young to appreciate it then, but when I think back to all the castles, beautiful gardens and artwork we saw over there, I had no idea that years later I would be studying the architecture and masterful artistry that surrounded me as a child.

Still, at that time my main interest in Germany was plain and simple; their wonderful assortment of candies like Coca Cola Gummies, Kinda Chocolate and "Nutella" to be exact. If you have ever been to Germany, you know exactly what I'm talking about. My mother had a friend named Troudell who worked at the Ferrero Chocolate Factory, and when we returned to the United States, she would send us a big box of all our favorite Ferrero candy for Christmas. Troudell was the best!

The rolling green countryside of Stuttgart, with its little postcard towns set in picturesque valleys, was a gift for the senses. I had never seen anything like that in Jersey. Although, unknown to most people, South Jersey is also pretty green. They don't call it "The Garden State" for nothing. Still, it could never compete with Germany's rich architecture, delectable foods, rolling hillsides, and history that spans thousands of years.

Unfortunately, along with the adventures of a new land and the wonderful experiences we enjoyed in Germany, it proved to be a spiritual valley of dead man's bones for our family.

During our three-year stay in Germany, we moved to three different towns: Stuttgart, Darmstadt, and Geissen. I can count on one hand the amount of times we attended a church service, even though each army base we lived on had a couple to choose from. I didn't know what denomination they were, but I would see the buildings as we passed by from time to time. I never asked why we stopped going, and soon I didn't even notice the church buildings anymore. The three years would pass by quickly. During our third year there, our family experienced a series of strange and unfortunate events that would cause that year to be our last in Germany.

One morning I heard a loud sound like someone dropped a bowling ball outside my bedroom door. At once everyone ran from their bedrooms to see what caused the sound. When I looked inside the bathroom I saw my father shaking on the floor with his tongue hanging out of his mouth. Terrified, I ran back to my room in tears and fell to my knees to pray to God to "let my Daddy be okay." I found out later that he was having an epileptic seizure, and when he fell he broke his shoulder. Then a couple months later my father would also be diagnosed with diabetes. The diabetes would develop into diabetic neuropathy, which affected the nerves in his legs and caused him to be confined to a wheel chair for the rest of his life. Of course, this would cause my father to have to retire after twenty-six years of service in the Army. This was quite a blow to him and our family, which caused me to remember the God I learned about at church
years ago, and ask Him for help.

Back To The World

Soon we were on our way back to "The World". That's how Americans in Germany referred to the United States. We called the U.S. "The World" because to us "Army Brats," the United States was where everything was available. Germany wasn't laden with all the little luxuries that we had back in the U.S.

When we returned to "The World," we moved to Fort Bragg, North Carolina. It was a short stint that only lasted for about one year, but it was worth it to witness the marching band at EE Smith High School. If you're from the south, you know that you don't go to the football games to watch the game (although the football team was really good too), you go to watch the band! After enjoying the hot summer sun of North Carolina, we finally moved back to LaGorce Square, where I had spent the first nine years of my life. It was an exciting reunion with many of my friends who were still there.

I remember my first day back to school. I was in ninth grade and as soon as my old friends saw me, they recognized me and exclaimed, "T, I can't believe you are back!" It was a great feeling to know that they were as excited to see me, as I was to see them. So there I sat, the new kid in class once again. This was a feeling that I was all too familiar with, having moved five times in the last four years. But this time it was different. This time I was home.

But when it came to my spiritual nourishment, I was starving to death.

Once again, I was living in the same neighborhood where Reverend Venerable, who took us to Saint Mary's Methodist Church, used to live. But unfortunately, he was no longer there, and we never made it back to Saint Mary's. I can remember riding by the church building and seeing that it was still there, but we never ventured back inside. The symptoms of our family's spiritual depravity continued to get worse in the coming years.

Two years later, we would move again to a town a few miles away from our original hometown. I was now in the eleventh grade and in the process of making new friends, some good, some not so good. Needless to say, there was still no spirituality or exposure to the Bible taking place in my life. My spiritual growth seemed to stop when I was nine years old.

I'll never forget one morning when I was a junior in high school. I headed out early to a neighbor's house so we could walk to school together. In my immature and dysfunctional naiveté, this was a particularly exciting morning, due to our plan to drink some beer and smoke some marijuana, that he got from his brother, on our way to school. So sure enough, as we took the thirty-minute walk to school down our neighborhood streets at 7:00 AM, that's exactly what we did.

Needless to say, we made total fools of ourselves that day, with everyone knowing that we were drunk and high. Of course, we thought it made us look cool and daring. Unfortunately, coming back to "The World" had its pros and cons. The cons were that my life began to be filled with several negative things that this world had to offer. I was heading down a path of destruction being laid out for me by the prince of darkness himself, encouraging my bad decisions in hope of throwing me headlong into a deadly spiral of dysfunction.

Then, something powerful happened my senior year of high school that would affect the rest of my life. For years I had a knack for doodling and drawing various things. Of course, I never thought anything of it. Although, it did cause me to take an art class in my senior year, mainly because I thought it would be an easy A. After designing an album cover (remember those?), a couple logos, and a few full page advertisements, my art teacher Mr. Dretch noticed I was a natural when it came to designing and said three words to me that changed my life. He said, "You have talent," and suggested I go to an art school in Philadelphia after graduation. I gave the suggestion serious consideration because I loved being creative and didn't really have any other plans after graduation. Still, to think that I had enough talent to get into a school that is specifically for people who are gifted at designing and creating art? That was as crazy to me as a rooster wearing socks. Still, it gave me a direction where there once was none. So I began to listen more closely to Mr. Dretch and let him prepare me for a possible career in commercial art.

Sure, my mom gave me kudos as a kid whenever I brought something home from school that I created, but no one ever told me I was good enough to go to art school and become a professional graphic designer until Mr. Dretch did. His confidence in me was all it took for me to believe that I had what it took to make this new found purpose a reality. As my final year of high school progressed, Mr. Dretch helped me apply to several schools of art. I was pleasantly surprised to be accepted by several of them. The one closest to home was across the bridge in Philly, so after graduating from Willingboro High School in 1982, I was on my way to the Art Institute of Philadelphia.

Schools of Art

My experience at the Art Institute was exhilarating! The school took up three floors of a high rise on Chestnut Street in the heart of Center City Philadelphia. The environment was electric with movies like "Trading Places" being shot around the corner at the "Cloths Pin" (I actually saw Dan Aykroyd and Eddie Murphy from a short distance), and talented designers from around the region, eager to display their creative chops. It presented a competitive and energetic atmosphere in class that I just couldn't get enough of.

The only down side was at that time the Art Institute was only a two-year program. Since I wanted to eventually have a bachelor's degree, after one year at the Art Institute, I transferred to Temple University's Tyler School of Art in Elkins Park, just outside Philadelphia. I would be the first person in my family to get a college degree if I made it all the way through, so I was determined to do well.

After commuting for a semester, I moved into an apartment just off campus and became more serious about becoming a graphic designer, but at the same time I took part in the partying that goes on at most colleges, continuing to drink on the weekends, smoking pot, and even trying cocaine on one occasion. Spiritually, I was lost, living according to how I saw others around me living. My personality and character were being shaped by the world. I was basically a reflection of the dysfunction and toxicity that plagued my family and society in general. My standards of morality were depleted. Yet, it was cool because the crowd said it was. Still, I had no concept or knowledge of God's will for my life. Unfortunately, the darkness in my life began to manifest itself in occasional bouts of depression and despair. That's when I found an outlet through writing.

I enrolled in a couple poetry courses at Tyler and found it to be a way for me to express exactly what I was feeling. My professor S. Sanchez was amazing at teaching her students to draw out their emotions and pour them into the written page. I soon realized that much of what I wrote about consisted of how miserable I was. My life consisted of trying to please others and escape reality, which left me feeling as fake as a mannequin in a storefront window, looking out onto a callous world.

Although I was still pursuing my goal to be a great graphic designer, my purpose and motivation for life itself began to wane, which led me to a dreadful day during my junior year at Tyler. It was actually a sunny day, but the sun had not yet penetrated my soul, and darkness surrounded my countenance as I made my way to a bench outside my apartment. Sitting alone, overwhelmed by feelings of hopelessness and despair, my heart began to look back at younger days of joy and unabated enthusiasm, days when my heart was not heavy with the weight of counterfeit reality and false affection.

As the position of my head betrayed my efforts to recapture a positive outlook on my life, I considered for a brief moment what the world would be like without me. What if I no longer existed in this physical reality? What if I no longer allowed the callous claws of this ravenous world the freedom to scratch at my weaknesses, as the raven does the road kill that has been left to rot in the midday sun? And what of those who do love me, like my mother? What hurt would I cause them, if I should end my life? Will I simply become a victim of the dysfunctions that have beset me in my prior days? Should I allow the darkness within me to win? It was at this pinnacle of decision that I believe God placed within my mind a memory.

I remembered a loving and compassionate friend that I had learned about at that Vacation Bible School years ago when I was a child. His name was Jesus. I remembered how He performed miracles in the lives of people who were sick or had deadly diseases. How He healed a blind man and caused him to see. How He healed a paralyzed man and made him able to walk. My eyes glazed over with tears of despair, I did something I had not done since I was a child: I prayed to God. In my prayer I said, "Jesus, if you are who you said you were in the Bible, and you actually did those miracles that the Bible records, then I need you to do one for me. I need you to give me purpose and joy in my life. I have tried, and I can't do this life on my own." Then I said, "Amen" at the end because I had heard other people in the past do that at the end of prayers. And

I left it at that. It wasn't anything too long and drawn out. Plus, I was almost late for class, so I dried my eyes, picked up my stuff, and went on to my painting class.

About two weeks went by, and I was still pretty miserable, but then I saw it. Someone had posted a flyer about a Bible study that would take place on campus on Tuesday nights. It caught my attention, and I started thinking about attending. It had been approximately twelve years since I had seen a Bible or learned about God. Still, the thought of seeking whether this "God stuff" and the Bible was legit, was very intriguing to me. When the following Tuesday rolled around, there I was in a room of people with Bibles, saying hello to each other and conversing. I didn't know any of them, so I just took a seat and waited for the study to start. Soon after I sat down, an older guy came over, introduced himself to me, and welcomed me to the study.

Come to find out, he was a graduate student and the leader of the Bible study. He started out by talking about creation and how God created the earth and all its inhabitants in six days, according to the beginning of the book of Genesis. Other people began to chime in as the discussion grew around the subject of creation. After about forty-five minutes, the study was over and everyone was standing and talking. I said hello to a few people, and we exchanged names and talked for a few minutes. But I wasn't all that comfortable, so I left pretty quickly after the study was over. But the discussion we had got me thinking about God and this amazing world we live in.

In His Image

Being a graphic design major, there was one thing that I remembered learning about God and His relationship with mankind when I was a kid in church. It was that God was creative. I remember the Bible teacher talking about God's creation process in Genesis and saying that God made us "in His image." I didn't quite understand exactly what that meant when I was younger. But now I was beginning to get it. The amazing and wonderful thing about being a designer is the fact that I can have a thought, that is intangible, existing only in my mind, and bring it into my physical world. When I thought about it more, I began to realize that one of the ways being made in the "image of God" is manifested in us as humans is through our ability to have an idea or thought, which is actually spiritual in nature, and make it become part of our physical reality.

I began to look around at the buildings and physical items in my apartment and classrooms, as well as the fantastic designs and artwork my friends and fellow designers were creating. Each time I did So I had no choice but to accept that they all began with an intangible thought, something that could not be grasped physically until it was made with the physical elements provided to us in this physical world.

So in my limited understanding, I ventured to say that the only difference between mankind and God is that we have to use the physical elements in our world to bring our thoughts into existence. Yet, in our Tuesday Bible study, we talked about how God "spoke" all things into existence. Of course, as a child, I thought that was pretty far-fetched. But when I thought about it more logically, in relation to my own ability to create and design things that begin with an intangible thought in my mind, I realized that God had a thought, and being in essence the highest manifestation of thought, was able to create physical reality through the power of His mind and spoken word. I know this was pretty deep contemplation for someone who wasn't even sure that he believed and understood God. Still, after talking about God creating our physical world, it became logically evident that we have a similar ability to bring our thoughts into our reality and make them tangible items in our physical world. Could this be one of the ways we are "made in His image?"

This concept became an obsession for me as I walked throughout the Tyler School of Art campus and examined more closely the trees, squirrels, and birds along my path, considering their intricate designs, only to be humbled by their magnificence and the realization that I wouldn't have a clue how to create something as amazing as them. Yet, someone or something had to have had the intelligence and power to create them, because there they were, an amazing design with function, purpose, and beauty.

As I contemplated these things over the next few days, my faith in a Divine Designer began to grow, simply by observing nature and creation around me. I began to wonder why every designer wasn't a believer in a Divine Designer. How arrogant could mankind be to think that we designed ourselves? Considering how extremely sophisticated the design of the human body is, why isn't every doctor a believer in a Divine Creator? Don't they see how sophisticated the design of the human body is?

Of course, I couldn't keep this new revelation inside, so I started sharing some of my thoughts with my friends at school. Some of them thought I was becoming religious and didn't want anything to do with it. As for me, it wasn't about being religious. I wasn't attaching myself to any religious organization. I was simply using basic logic and the realities that were present in our physical world to show myself and others that there is a design and logic to all that we see in nature.

Some of my other friends thought what I was talking about was interesting. One of them told me this story. He wasn't sure if it was true or not, but it related to what we were discussing about there being design and purpose in creation. He stated that, at one point, Ben Franklin created a physical model of the solar system. (Going to school at Temple University in Philadelphia, Ben was not only an American hero, but a hometown favorite). The story goes that he presented the model to some of his colleagues. When an additional colleague walked in the room late, he asked Ben, "Who created this?" Ben was said to have sarcastically replied, "No one, it created itself." We both chuckled at the sarcasm. But we knew that it takes more faith to believe that all the design we see around us could "just happen," than it does to admit that it must have an intelligent author and designer.

All this talk and contemplation about a Divine Creator got me thinking really hard about going back to the Bible study on Tuesday nights in Tyler Hall. So there I was again the following Tuesday, saying hello to a few familiar faces as others introduced themselves to me. Everyone was very cool and made me feel comfortable being there. That night I would find out that the graduate student who was leading the study was a member of the Catholic Church. I also found out that the rest of the people attending the study considered themselves to be "Born-Again Christians." I wasn't sure what that meant, but I was open to learn more about it. Over a few weeks, we entered into some very interesting discussions regarding the Bible and various topics within it. After the third meeting, I decided to buy my own Bible and seek out a local church in the area on my own. I thought about attending one of the churches that my Bible study friends went to, but I wasn't sure if I wanted to be a "Born-Again Christian" or a "Catholic." Although, I did want to find out more about the Bible, so I looked in the

Yellow Pages (remember those?) and found a church very close to Tyler's campus.

The Sinner's Prayer

The church that I began attending every Sunday was called "New Covenant Church." It didn't seem to have any specific church affiliation like Catholic or Baptist, and it was made up of predominately African Americans. The one thing I enjoyed about the church service at Saint Mary's, when I was a child, was the music. This New Covenant Church must have felt the same way, because they not only had a pianist to accompany the singing, but also a drummer, bass player, lead guitarist, and saxophonist as well. Since I used to play around on my own drum set when I was a kid, this church was the place for me on Sunday mornings.

After attending there for approximately one year, I went forward when they had their altar call for those who want to be saved and accept Christ as their personal Savior. By doing so, it was understood that those who responded would become Born-Again Christians." When I first met my "born-again" friends at Tyler, I wasn't sure if I wanted to be like them, but by this time I had heard several sermons about Jesus dying for me, becoming the sacrifice that God required in order for me to be forgiven of my sins and be born again according to

John 3:3. I also knew that I had plenty of sins that needed to be forgiven. So when the minister gave the altar call, I went forward, along with a few other people. The minister greeted each of us and told us how glad he was that we came forward to accept Christ.

The church gave up a resounding applause for those of us who had come to the altar. As the band struck up another song as those who came forward were escorted to a room in the back to meet up with spiritual counselors. I was instructed to sit down in front of another man as he asked me if I believe that Jesus is the Son of God, and that He died for my sins. I replied, "Yes." Then he asked me if I was willing to accept Him as my personal Savior, and again I replied, "Yes." He then bowed his head to pray and asked me to bow my head also and repeat after him.

I repeated something like, *"Jesus I accept you with all my heart as my Lord and Savior. I believe that You are the Son of God that you died for my sins and rose from the dead. I dedicate my life to You. Amen."* What I learned later was that the prayer I had just finished praying was known as the "Sinner's Prayer." After we prayed, he shook my hand and congratulated me on being a Born-Again Christian." A smile quickly grew within my face and I was so thankful to God for loving me and saving me from going to an eternal hell. Then I thought, *Wow! I'm a Born-Again Christian!* I couldn't wait to tell my family and friends.

The next chance I got, I went home to share the good news that I "got saved" and now was a "Born-Again Christian." My homecoming was well received. Although my family did not know much about being "Born Again," they knew it had to do with Christianity, so they were happy for me. One highlight of my return home to share about my new faith in Jesus was when I went to see one of my best friends from childhood. When I told him about being saved, he told me that he had accepted Christ as his Savior as well. At that point we hugged, rejoiced, and talked of how Jesus saved us from a life of sin and despair.

Shortly thereafter I noticed that the curse words that so easily rolled off my tongue in previous years were, for the most part, no longer present among my speech. The drug and alcohol use was also absent from my weekends, as I chose to hang out with my Christian friends instead of hitting the usual keg party or night club in town. The promiscuous lifestyle was no longer part of who I was either. Still, perhaps the most recognizable change that I noticed in my life after accepting Christ as my personal savior was that my thoughts of despair and lack of self-worth had turned to joy, hope, and purpose. When I returned to college after my summer break, I went to the next Tuesday Night Bible Study and shared with them how I got saved. They were all excited for me, except for the Catholic guy. He didn't quite understand the whole "Born-Again" thing until we explained it to him. A week or so after that, I met some other Born-Again friends on campus. One of them was a member of a contemporary Christian band and asked me if I could play an instrument. I told her that I played around on the drums a little when I was a kid and had an old set at home. "Cool," she exclaimed, "Would you like to come to our rehearsal?" she asked. "Sure, why not," I responded. "That sounds like fun!"

The Contemporary Christian band consisted of five members, all of who considered themselves to be Born-Again Christians. Come to find out, the band had everything they needed, except for a drummer. So they asked me to be in the band and I was pleased to accept. Since I still had my old drum set at my parent's house, I went home to get it and started practicing with the band in my spare time. After a few rehearsals, the leader of the group set up a few local gigs at churches in the area. He was even able to get us into one of the local theatres in Philadelphia. Our band was not that good, but to us, we were "praising the Lord" and sharing His word. That's all that mattered.

Unfortunately, as time went on, the personal lives of some of the members of the band were very inconsistent with what we were preaching and singing about. One of the members got pregnant by another band member. It wasn't long before everyone became discouraged, and eventually the group broke up. It was probably a good thing because, as I grew in my knowledge of the Bible, I learned something very interesting about spiritual music under the New Covenant and in the New Testament.

The Berean Church

Upon graduating from college, I moved to Atlantic City, New Jersey, which was about an hour and a half away from my parent's home. That's right, I was on my way to "Sin City." Well, at least the East Coast version, anyway. This was my first real job out of college. I worked for Van Wagner Advertising, an Ad Agency based out of New York City. Van Wagner was responsible for operating Resorts Casino's animated billboard on the boardwalk. They hired me to create various animated advertisements for display on the billboard. It was my first time working with animation. Once I saw my artwork move, I was hooked. All I wanted to be from that point on was an animator and designer of motion graphics.

And I was also a Born-Again Christian now, so one of the first things I did when I got down there was to seek out a non-denominational church where I could worship. Although, this time I was looking for something a little more mellow. I would end up at a small church where the members patterned themselves after the Bereans in Acts 17, who *"searched the scriptures daily to find if these things were so."* The Bereans in Acts 17 wanted to see if the Apostle Paul was preaching things according to the Scriptures, so they searched the Scriptures to see if what he was preaching and teaching was true. I really liked that idea of searching the Scriptures for the truth, so I began worshipping there with them on Sundays and going to Bible study on Wednesday nights. I developed many new friends there and became one of the regulars. I found out that all of my friends there had also become Born-Again Christians by praying and accepting Jesus as their personal Savior.

Once a year, during the summer, all the church members would get together for a big picnic at a nearby lake. Along with the picnic, there would be swimming, water skiing, and other fun activities. Since the picnic was at a lake, the church leaders thought it would be an appropriate time to baptize any of those who wanted to be baptized in the lake by the minister. Everyone in the church, including myself, believed that baptism was not necessary for salvation, and that we were saved the minute we accepted Jesus as our Savior. Still, the minister taught us that baptism was an "outward showing of an inward grace." That it was something we should eventually do as followers of Christ, but that it was not necessary for our soul's salvation.

The first year I was a member at the Berean Church I was one of those baptized at the annual picnic. I felt good about being immersed in the water, although I knew that I was already saved before being baptized. We were simply following the example of Jesus, who was baptized by John. And I was good with that.

At that time, I believed that once I was saved I would always be saved. That's what I had been taught, although I never studied it for myself. When I inquired about what others believed regarding the teaching of "once saved, always saved," their belief was the same as mine, that if a person totally forsakes God after being "born again" then they were never really "born again" in the first place.

This was my understanding for several years until I eventually studied the topic in depth and found evidence that was contrary to my knowledge of the "once saved, always saved" doctrine. Here are some of the verses I found that either state or imply that it is possible for a person to fall away after being saved: Gal. 5:4, Romans 11:22, Hebrews 6:4-6.

My time in Atlantic City was short lived. I didn't realize how much of a ghost town that place became during the winter. Talk about depressing. After a year or so I tossed in the towel (I thought I'd use a boxing term, since I used to create all the boxing advertisements for Resorts on the animated billboard), and moved back to Willingboro with Mom and Dad.

That's when I started my own Graphic Design and Animation business called Motion Graphix. Since the Philadelphia Phillies and Eagles were operating the same type of sign at Veterans Stadium that I worked on for Van Wagner Advertising in Atlantic City, I called them up and got an interview to show them the work I did for Van Wagner. They liked my work and hired me as a freelance animator to create fan-oriented animations and advertisements for their scoreboard.

"Greg G"

It wasn't too long after being home that I hooked up with my former rap partner Greg Sprowl, also known as "Greg G." He was the other half of the rap group we had in high school called "The Awesome Two." We called ourselves a rap group, but we really only had one rap song, titled "Are You Ready For This?" And it wasn't even a whole song. We just had a few verses for each of us. Still, don't you know we would rap those few verses like no bodies business? Then of course we would laugh hysterically, thinking we were the best rap duo on the planet.

That was one thing about Greg G though, he was always laughing and having a good time. You could tell that Greg came from a good home, filled with a lot of love and laughter. The other thing I liked about him was that there was never a foul word heard coming from his mouth. His jovial and gregarious nature showed that he was very happy from within. I fancied myself to be quite the comedian as well. But there was something different about Greg. His joy was more authentic.

It was approximately seven years after our high school days, and his personality hadn't changed a bit. We started hanging out with each other again, playing basketball, rapping, playing card games, etc. While we hung out, we would sometimes talk about spiritual things. Knowing that Greg and his family went to church, occasionally he would bring up certain Bible verses that were very interesting. So I would write them down and read them when I got home. Sometimes I didn't have to wait until I got home, because Greg seemed to always have a Bible in his house and in his car. Who carries a Bible around in their car with them? But that was Greg G. He was all about the word of God.

As we shared a lot of our religious experiences with each other, what impressed me about Greg was that he seemed to always have an answer straight from the Bible. Those types of answers were hard to come by from the religious people I had encountered in the past. I was growing weary of all the posturing, performing, and emotionalism at the churches I had attended. When he offered an invitation to worship with him on Sunday, I gladly accepted in hopes of having a better experience.

That next Sunday I drove over to his house and followed him and his family to the church they attended, about thirty minutes away. We came upon a church building and a white sign with black letters that read, "church of Christ". The church building was small and quaint, with no more than 50 members in attendance. This was tiny compared to what I was used to. We were there in time for the Bible study before worship and I can remember hearing things being taught that were very intriguing. Between the Bible study and worship service, I was introduced to several members and many introduced themselves to me. Soon it was time for worship and we all sat down to hear some announcements and begin singing church songs.

The first thing that hit me in the face like a mud pie was the absence of a choir and instruments up front to sing along with. All they had was a man with a hymnbook, leading the entire church in *a cappella* singing. At this point I was beginning to feel sorry for this church, thinking that maybe they couldn't afford a piano and an organist. Thinking to myself, I said, "No wonder there is hardly anyone here; this place is dead. Where is the Spirit, the clapping, the shouts of praise, and the instruments?" I was in totally unfamiliar territory and began to think that these folks were weird.

After singing a couple songs, we had the Lord's Supper, which is when you eat the cracker and drink the grape juice. I had done this before in other churches, so I was familiar with it. Then came the sermon. The preacher was pretty good and used a lot of scripture references in his lesson, but before I knew it, the worship service was over and people were standing, talking, and laughing together. So I looked at Greg and said, "That's it?" He said, "Yup! Why do you ask?" I replied, "Because at my church, we would just be warming up." He laughed and went on to introduce me to a few more members of the church.

On the way home, I began to tell G the impression I got from his church, but he was quick to inform me that it wasn't "his church," but rather "Christ's church." "That's why we call it the church of Christ," he explained "according to Romans

16:16." That made sense to me, but I had to tell him the truth about my impression of their worship service. "Dude, you folks are dead!" I exclaimed, "Where is the spirit? I mean, it was kind of boring, Bruh. Sorry, but I'm just being honest." He laughed and took it very well, saying that he thought I might react that way, knowing the types of churches I had attended in the past. Still, he did not get offended, but continued to give me biblical answers for everything they taught and practiced. With every scripture he mentioned, I did my best to make a mental note or write it down, so I could check it out at another time.

__Baptism__

On another sunny Saturday, while Greg and I were coming from the basketball court, he saw how interested I had become in studying God's word and asked me if I had ever been baptized before? I was all too proud to respond with an emphatic "Yes, Sir, I have! It was when I worked in Atlantic City." I explained, "The church got together once a year at a lake for a picnic, and the minister baptized me in the lake." "In a lake?" Greg responded with intrigue, "That must have been pretty cool?" To which I replied, "Is that (cool) meaning cold, or (cool) meaning cool?" After laughing at our corniness, which we did quite often, he clarified that he meant "cool" as in "interesting."

His next question caught me off guard, when he asked, "What was the purpose of your baptism?" I wasn't sure where he was coming from, so I asked, "What do you mean?" And he replied, "I'm just wondering why you got baptized?" At first, I thought this was a trick question, but quickly realized that he was serious. So I tried my best to give him an honest answer.

"Well, because it was a way for me to show my faith and obedience to Christ. And since Jesus did it, we should do it too, right? It's an outward showing of an inward grace," I exclaimed, basically repeating what I learned at the Berean Church. I also knew that some churches baptize their members in order to become a member of that specific denomination, similar to the Baptist Church, so I thought maybe he's thinking along those lines. At that point he suggested I check out a few verses on the subject of baptism and began writing them down on a scrap piece of paper. I was willing to check them out, but I said to him, "What's the big deal? It doesn't have anything to do with my salvation." He just smiled and said, "Check out the verses and let me know what you think." Taking the verses from his hand, I became ever more anxious to see what he was talking about. So as soon as I got home, had taken a shower and eaten dinner, I started studying the subject of baptism. What I found was very interesting, to say the least.

One of the scriptures he wrote down was Mark 16:16 which quotes Jesus, after His resurrection, saying to the Apostles, *"anyone who believes and is baptized will be saved..."* But I knew in my heart that I was saved the second I accepted Jesus as my personal Savior. And that was way before being baptized. I mean, things in my life had changed drastically, so when I got saved, I knew it was the real deal!

So the next Sunday I confronted Greg saying, "Are you trying to tell me that a person isn't saved unless they are dunked in water?" Again, with a smile, he answered, "I never said that." I continued, "I hope you don't think water baptism has anything to do with a person's salvation" I argued as we walked into Bible class. "Because Romans 10:9 says, *"confess with your mouth and you will be saved."* Of course that was a quick paraphrase, but he knew what I was referring to. "That's a good verse," he replied. "Let's talk more about this after class." Although I knew that we should, since the class was about to begin, I was still agitated and wanted to get down to the bottom of this water baptism stuff.

So after class I wasn't about to let him off the hook, "What about Romans 10:9, Bruh?" I asked again. Much to my surprise, he didn't go into trying to explain away the verse, but simply said, "Keep on reading. There's more in that passage than you realize. God's truth is not about one verse in the bible, but all of the verses that pertain to a certain subject. So do yourself a favor and read all of Romans chapter 10," and I promise you, we will circle back around to Romans 10:9 after you check out the other verses I gave you earlier." Then, before we parted ways, he reiterated that he never said that baptism had anything to do with being saved, but that I developed that thought on my own by reading the scripture in the Bible. He was obviously suggesting that I was getting my thoughts from the scriptures themselves, not from him.

As we did our famous hand shake, as we always did when we came together or left each other, I let him know that I was going to fight this tooth and nail, because I knew for a fact that water baptism was not necessary for my salvation. Sure, I had been wrong about some spiritual things in the past, but this one was a no-brainer. Of course Ephesians 2:8, Romans 10:9-10 and the "thief on the cross" were verses that I hung my "faith only" hat upon. They told me plain and simple that all it takes is a person to believe in Christ in order to be saved. Although I tried to keep it cool, I still had to tell him as I walked toward my car that he was buggin' about baptism (You have to be an African American in the early 90s, in New Jersey to understand the term "buggin'." It's similar to "trippin'" or simply acting weird, to put it bluntly). And as only Greg-G could do, he belted out a gregarious laugh and yelled so I could hear him, as I was about to get into my car, "Check out the rest of those verses!" "Yeah, yeah, I will, I will," I responded with a smile in my voice.

I know Greg wanted me to study the first set of verses he gave me first, but I still couldn't get Romans 10:9 out of my head, so I did what he suggested and read the whole chapter. I found out that the Apostle Paul was writing to Christians who were members of the church in Rome. Then I finally got to my favorite verse, Romans 10:9, which states: *"That if you confess with your mouth the Lord Jesus and believe in your heart that God has raised Him from the dead, you will be saved..."* period! What more was there for me to know? I believed and confessed, and now I'm saved! But as I continued to read, as Greg encouraged me to do, the Lord showed me something very thought provoking.

The next verse, Romans 10:10 stated: *"For with the heart one believes unto salvation"* (NKJV). Other translations use the word "to" instead of "unto" (NAS). Either way, the word "unto" stuck out like a sore thumb. Was this verse saying that, if a person confesses and believes, then they are coming "unto" or "to" salvation, meaning there is still something to do before being saved? I didn't claim to know a whole lot, but I did know that Ephesians 2:8 clearly stated that we are *"not saved by works,"* But I had to get to the bottom of this subject, so I kept on studying.

In Romans 10:10, the NIV translation states that by believing and confessing, you "are saved." That's a different translation, but seemed to be more accurate, if you asked me. Still, I wanted to find out which translation was more consistent with the rest of the Bible. So I went to my other favorite scripture (Luke 23:39-43). Surely it would provide the powerful truth I needed to blow this baptism theory out of the water (no pun intended). All the thief on the cross had to do was believe and Jesus said he would be in paradise with Him. "No baptism needed here, right?" At least that's what I said to Greg the next time I saw him. But he brought a few things to my attention that I had to consider.

The first point was, although the thief would die after Jesus, after He made that statement on the cross about the thief being with Him in paradise, He and the thief were technically still under the Mosaic Law and Old Covenant. Baptism into Christ was not part of the Old Covenant system. They looked forward to Christ's atoning death on the cross, but His death had not yet taken place.

Another valid point he showed me was, for the thief on the cross to be in paradise with Jesus, his sins had to be forgiven. And of course Jesus had the power to forgive sins. No one that I know of today has that same power. When Jesus healed the lame man He said, *"but that you may know that the Son of Man has the power to forgive sins, take up your bed and walk" (Matt. 9:4-6)*. Since only God can forgive sins, and Jesus was God in the flesh (John 1:1, 14), He had the authority to forgive the thief's sins at any time or place. That was an interesting point that I hadn't heard before.

Taking these thoughts into consideration, I realized something. It was the fact that I wasn't hanging next to Jesus on a cross, but was living almost two thousand years after the death of Jesus. So the question in my mind was, "What is God's plan for people living today? If Jesus is not here to say, "Your sins are forgiven," how do we receive the forgiveness of our sins? As far as I knew, it was simply by believing that Jesus was the Son of God and that He died for our sins.

This study was starting to get really juicy as I continued studying the verses that Greg gave me at the onset of this whole discussion. The next one was Matthew 28:18 where Jesus said, *"All authority in heaven and on earth has been given to Me. Go therefore and make disciples of all nations, baptizing them in the name of the Father and of the Son and of the Holy Spirit, teaching them to observe all things I have commanded you."* I could have been wrong, but it actually sounded to me like Jesus was saying in this verse that baptizing someone was part of making them a disciple of Christ.

Still, that couldn't be right, so I went on to the next verse, which was Acts 2:38, where Peter said to *"repent and be baptized for the forgiveness of your sins."* Now this verse seemed to suggest that baptism was part of being forgiven of your sins, a prerequisite for being saved. I also knew that God would not contradict Himself, so I had to dig deeper into His word to find out exactly what God means regarding belief, faith, baptism and salvation. I prayed earnestly for God to show me the truth regarding these subjects, and dove head first into an intense study on God's plan of salvation.

One thing I noticed about that previous verse was that Peter didn't say anything about believing in Christ, but only to "repent and be baptized for the remission (forgiveness) of sins." Without panicking, I continued to read through the chapter and found that verse 47 of Acts 2 stated, *"the Lord added to their number daily, those who were being "saved."* Were they being saved by repenting and being baptized? Of course, I knew of Isaiah 59:1-2, that sin separates us from God, so being baptized "for the forgiveness of sins" was something I wanted to know more about.

But I still was not convinced that I needed to be dunked in water for the forgiveness of my sins, in order to be saved. How could God include a "work" like water baptism as part of the salvation process, when verses like John 3:16 and others say that all a person needs to do to be saved from eternal damnation is to believe in Jesus? Was God being inconsistent? I knew that could not be the case, so I had to continue seeking His truth. I know that if I seek, then I will find. So I looked up other verses having to do with baptism and the history of how other people became Christians in the New Testament.

Much to my surprise, I found out that Mark 16:16, the first verse Greg gave me, in which Jesus states, *"whoever believes and is baptized shall be saved,"* is not found in all Bible translations. My Bible's concordance had a footnote, which stated that the earlier manuscripts did not contain this verse and suggested that it was added years later after the original manuscript had been written.

You will not believe the adulation I experienced! These people were trying to create a doctrine based on a few verses, one that some say isn't even supposed to be in the Bible! Yeah, now my research was coming together to support what I had believed all along, that I didn't need to be baptized in order to be saved. I couldn't wait to call Greg and tell him what I had found.

"Yo G! It's Tommie. What's going on?" I asked as we began our phone conversation. "Tommie Lee The Third! What's up Man?" To which I responded, "It's all good." Continuing with glee in my voice, I said, "Hey, I found out that the first verse you gave me isn't even supposed to be in the bible, according to my concordance. What's up with that?" I asked. "Yeah," he responded in a calm voice, "there are several verses that are from the later manuscripts, but they are still considered inspired by God. If you don't like that one, read Acts chapter eight, beginning with verse 26 and see what happened with the Ethiopian Eunuch." "Ok" I said, "I'll take a look. Hey, did you check out the Sixers game last night? My boys are lookin' good…"

<u>The Ethiopian Eunuch</u>

I was familiar with the story of the Ethiopian Eunuch, but I wanted to read it again to see if I had missed anything. So the next chance I got, I sat down and read Acts chapter 8. Philip was sent over to a Eunuch who was in charge of Queen Candace's treasure, and was riding in a chariot, reading from the book of Isaiah. Philip asked him if he understood what he was reading and the Eunuch replied, *"How can I unless someone guides me."* Philip did exactly that. The Bible states that Philip *"began at that same verse and preached unto him Jesus."* When they came to some water, the Eunuch said, *"Here is water, what should hinder me from being baptized?"* Then they stopped the chariot and they both went *"down into the water and he baptized him."* When they came up out of the water, it says that the Eunuch *"went on his way, rejoicing."* Ok, the story was as I remembered it to be, but this time the Eunuch's baptism stuck out like a red flag.

You can probably imagine what my question was to myself at this point. "Why didn't Philip tell

42

him to pray a prayer to accept Christ as his Savior? Some texts do include that the Eunuch said, "I believe that Jesus is the Son of God." But how did the Eunuch know about water baptism when the Bible says that Philip simply *"preached unto him Jesus?"* My unwanted conclusion was that Philip must have told him something about water baptism when he *"preached unto him Jesus."* It could not have been Holy Spirit baptism he preached to him. If so, they would have ridden right past the water.

Of course, Peter could have taught him that baptism was his first act of obedience after accepting Christ as his personal Savior and being saved (a teaching I had heard previously). Still, it certainly sounded consistent with what Peter said in Acts 2:38, to be *"baptized for the forgiveness of sins."* But for the life of me, I couldn't get behind this water baptism stuff. What if someone wanted to be saved in the middle of a desert? That's why you can't make water baptism a requirement for salvation. If you do, tons of people would never be able to become Christians, because there's no water!

Wait a minute. Let me rethink that for a second. I just read about someone who was in the desert, seeking the truth, and God sent a preacher from miles away to teach him the truth about Jesus, and then provided water after he had heard the gospel, for him to be baptized. Could God provide the means today to someone who is truly seeking to be saved? Could it be true that my sins would not be forgiven unless I was immersed in water for the forgiveness of my sins? That still didn't sound right to me. I needed more confirmation, so I kept praying and seeking out more truth on the matter.

Paul's Conversion

Because the account of the Ethiopian Eunuch was so intriguing, I continued to read in Acts 9, and encountered the story of the Apostle Paul. This was another familiar story to me and another one that I thought supported the "faith only" teaching. From what I remembered, Saul was converted on his way to Damascus when he spoke to Jesus. This time I read it for myself a little closer and found that Saul was on his way to bind Christians in Damascus and bring them back to Jerusalem. On his way he saw a bright light that blinded him and heard a voice saying, *"Saul, why are you persecuting me?"* What Saul said in response to the voice was jarring to me this time around. It was my understanding previously that Saul confessed Jesus as his Lord. But in verse 5 of Acts chapter 9, Saul asked the question, *"Who are you Lord?"* Are you serious? You mean to tell me that Saul had no idea who he was calling *"Lord?"* At least not until Jesus responded and said, *"I am Jesus whom you are persecuting."*

For years I was taught that Saul confessed Jesus as his Lord because Saul addressed the voice that was speaking to him as "Lord." But if that's the reasoning, did anyone ever notice that the three previous words before the word "Lord" are "who are you?" Obviously, Saul knew it was someone in authority speaking to him. It's not every day that you get knocked off your horse and become blind. Yet, anyone in a position of authority could have been called "Lord" at that time. Even Magistrates and husbands were called "Lord" in early history (1 Peter 3:6). So that caused me to think that, even if Saul did think it was God speaking to him, he certainly didn't know it was Jesus at first, especially because he was on his way to imprison those who were followers of Jesus.

Of course, we can assume that Saul believed in the authority and power of Jesus after becoming blind, but it's debatable whether he was "converted," when Saul asked, *"What do you want me to do, Lord?"* considering that he called Jesus "Lord" even when he didn't know who he was talking to. We also know that Jesus stated, *"Not everyone who calls me Lord, Lord, will enter the kingdom of heaven, but those who **do** the will of the Father..." (Matt. 7:21)*. Jesus responded to Saul's question, replying, *"Arise and go into the city, and you will be told what you **must do**."* It sounded to me like there was still something that Saul "must do" regarding his relationship with Jesus. After reading further, it seemed like that which Saul "must do" related to his conversion, and ultimately his salvation.

Wanting to know more, I followed Saul's story through the ninth chapter of Acts to where it talks of a man named Ananias, a disciple of Christ, who was told by the Lord to go to Saul and, help him receive his sight. Ananias went to Saul and laying his hands on him, said, *"Brother Saul, the Lord Jesus who appeared to you on the road as you came has sent me that you may receive your sight and be filled with the Holy Spirit. Immediately there fell from his eyes something like scales and he received his sight at once and he arose and was baptized" (Acts 9:18).* I understood Paul needing to be filled with the miraculous "power" of the Holy Spirit, as the twelve Apostles were (Acts 1:8, 2:1-4), but the "baptized" part at the end of that verse was very intriguing and caused me to dig deeper into fully understanding why Saul was baptized by Ananias.

My bible had a reference to Acts 22, so I turned over to it and found that Paul re-tells the story of what happened to him in Damascus. There were a couple things that I found very interesting about the Acts 22 account.

Firstly, it gives more information about who Ananias was in stating that he was a *"devout man according to the law, having a good testimony with all the Jews who dwelt there."* In other words, he was a Jew who had converted to Christ. You'll understand why I'm pointing this out in a minute.

Secondly, in the Acts 22 account of Saul's meeting with Ananias, he tells Saul to *"rise and be baptized and wash away your sins, calling on the name of the Lord."* Now, this was a powerful verse because it seemed to be stating clearly that being baptized was the method in which Saul would have

46

his sins washed away. And of course, I knew that being saved was all about being forgiven of one's sins, for *"in Christ we have forgiveness of sins" (Eph. 1:7).* So knowing the proper method that God prescribed for me to have my sins washed away was extremely important to me.

I already understood that sin has separated mankind from God according to several passages like Isaiah 59:1-2, and for me to enter into the presence of God for all eternity, I would have to have my sins forgiven. That's why this verse in Acts 22:16 jumped out at me like a bolt of lightning. Ananias said that Saul should *"be baptized and wash away your sins."* Was this to mean that water baptism, preceded by belief in Jesus for salvation, is how one's past sins are washed away and forgiven? I still didn't want to believe it. But I kept reading verse after verse that seemed to be saying that very thing. I also looked at the original Greek language and found out that the word "baptize" in the original Greek text was the word "baptiso" meaning to "immerse into a liquid," like that of a fabric being immersed in liquid dye to change its color. So the true biblical baptism that these verses were referring to was one where the person's entire body is immersed into water, not the sprinkling or pouring of water on the head that we commonly see as baptism today.

This was evident with the Ethiopian Eunuch, when it states that he and Phillip *"both went down into the water,"* and also *"came up out of the water" (Acts 8:38).* If a sprinkle on the head is good enough for baptism, then why would they both need to go down into the water? They could have stood by the bank and Phillip could have grabbed a handful of water, if total immersion wasn't necessary. But again, the Bible seems to be teaching something different from what many are practicing in the world today.

I had also heard from my "faith only" friends in the past the verse *"those who call on the name of the Lord shall be saved."* Many of them used that verse to base their belief in "calling Jesus their Savior" being all that's needed for their soul's salvation. I wasn't sure where that verse was, so I looked it up in my concordance.

I found it in Romans 10:13. It stated, *"whoever calls on the name of the Lord shall be saved."* Now, without having studied what I have been studying about baptism, I would have taken this verse at face value and concluded that when a person calls on Jesus for salvation, they are therefore saved. But when I put this verse together with Acts 22:16, and Saul's conversion, I saw that *"calling on the name of the Lord"* includes baptism, as Ananias said to Saul, *"Be baptized and wash away your sins, calling on the name of the Lord."* Wow! I was starting to see how important it is to know the whole Bible, and not just a few key verses.

So does this mean that a person actually calls upon the name of the Lord by being baptized for the forgiveness of their sins? I was beginning to see a pattern here among those who were being converted in the New Testament. It seemed consistent that

48

belief in Christ, followed by confession, repentance, and immersion in water for the forgiveness of sins, was what was taught by Jesus and the Apostles. Not to mention, this seemed to be the method in which they were added to God's church (Act 2:47).

But if baptism had to do with my salvation, and if it's that clear in the scriptures, (which I wasn't sure of yet), then why are there millions of people who consider themselves to be Christians, not teaching or practicing a water baptism for the forgiveness of sins? Are we being honest with God's word? That was the question burning within me.

Another teaching I used to hear regarding Paul's conversion was that when Ananias came to Saul, he called him "brother." "See that proves he was already a Christian, because Ananias was a Christian and he called him brother." Seriously, this was the teaching I used to hear. Looking at the scriptures closer, it seems to me that Ananias is referring more to his cultural "brotherhood" and "nationality" that he and Saul share as Jews.

I say that because, as I'm learning about this baptism stuff, I'm realizing that, if Saul (Paul) needed to be baptized for the forgiveness of his sins in order to be a true Brother in Christ, then Ananias was definitely talking in cultural terms and of their Jewish heritage when he referred to Saul as "brother," since Saul had not been baptized yet. Still, I wasn't totally convinced about all this stuff, so I bounced what I was learning off of Greg, who was excited to see me seeking out the truth about God's plan of salvation in His holy word.

Then came my next question. Although I had already been baptized, will it jeopardize my salvation, if my understanding of why I was being baptized was not as Ananias told Paul, "to wash away my sins"? Because I knew for a fact that when I got baptized in that river, I wasn't thinking that it was *"for the forgiveness of my sins,"* as Peter stated in Acts 2:38.

At the same time, I still couldn't get past how ridiculous it sounded that not being dunked in water will keep me out of heaven! With a grin, Greg responded to my angst, "I hear ya! Still, it sounds like you've learned some interesting things. Want to learn more?" he asked. He knew that my answer would be, "Of course, whatta ya got?" To which G replied, "Check out Acts 18 and 19 when you get a chance." So on to Acts 18 I went, the next chance I got, but before I went there I took a little detour.

A Better Understanding

During this period of searching, I discussed my questions with several friends, other than Greg. Some of them had a Baptist upbringing and others were another denomination or simply non-denominational born-again believers in Christ. Although the Baptists seemed to accept the teachings of baptism the most, even they did not see it as a prerequisite to being saved, but more so as an initiation ceremony for becoming a member of the Baptist Church. And if you look at the history of the Baptist Church, it was started by John Smyth in 1612, long after Jesus established His church in 33AD.

I wasn't sure whether water baptism is necessary for being forgiven and added to the Lord's church, but one thing I did know, I didn't want to be baptized into a church that someone other than Jesus established. This is what I saw in many of the denominations around me. The Lutheran Church was established by Martin Luther in 1522. The Presbyterian Church was established by John Calvin in 1702. The Methodist Church was established by John Wesley in 1784. The church I wanted to be a member of was the one that Jesus established in 33AD. The one that is recorded beginning in the bible, in Acts chapter 2.

As I looked closer at this subject in the New Testament, I saw that John the Baptist (or baptizer/immerser), a forerunner to Christ, was baptizing people in the Jordan river. It is said that his baptism was a *"baptism of repentance" (Mark 1:4).* So as the scriptures state, many came confessing their sins. John was baptizing them as they confessed their sins in repentance to God.

There were a couple other verses I found regarding John's baptism. Both of them said that John's baptism was also *"for the remission of sins."* That word "remission" was a little foreign to me, so I had to look it up. I found that it was basically another word for "forgiveness." As I dug deeper I found that John prepared the way for Jesus and the New Covenant by immersing people in the Jordan River *"for the forgiveness of sins."* In Luke 3:3, it states that, *"the word of God came to John, the son of Zacharias, in the wilderness. And he came into all the district around the Jordan, preaching a baptism of repentance for the forgiveness of sins."*

Being a Born-Again Christian, and having heard this verse talked about in sermons before, it was my understanding that the word "for" in Acts 2:38 meant "because of." In other words, Peter was not instructing the people to be baptized in order to be saved and have their sins forgiven, but more so "because of" having already been saved and forgiven of their sins.

When I discussed this with Greg, he encouraged me to get a bible reference book called Strong's Greek Concordance and look at the original language of this and other verses, to get a better understanding of their meaning through the original

Greek text. What I found would clear up a whole lot of biblical misunderstanding by millions of people who call themselves Christians.

The next chance I got, I headed over to the bookstore in the mall (remember those) to get myself a Strong's Concordance and looked up the 38th verse of Acts chapter 2.

I found that the word "of" in Acts 2:38, in the original Greek language, is the word "eis" meaning: "for," "to," "unto," and "toward." None of which were "because of." So then I started to get a little angry again, thinking to myself, *"You mean to tell me I've been duped again regarding a major biblical truth?"* Yet, at the same time, I was thankful that I was finding out the truth of the matter pertaining to Acts 2:38. So my next question was, where did the whole "because of" concept come from? For there to be millions of people (I'm guessing) who believe the "because of" theory, there has to be some biblical and grammatical foundation for it somewhere.

That's what led me to look up other verses on the "forgiveness (or remission) of sins" and see how they read in the original Greek language. Eventually I came across Matthew chapter 26 and verse 28. In this passage Jesus is partaking of the Passover Feast with the Apostles. This, of course is commonly known as "The Last Supper." I'm sure you've seen the famous painting by Leonardo Da Vinci. After Jesus took the cup and gave thanks, He gave it to His disciples, saying, *"drink all of it, for this is My blood of the new covenant, which is shed for many for the remission of sins"* (Matt. 26:28) Here we have it again, the same phrase as in Acts 2:38, *"for the remission of sins."* So I looked it up in Strong's concordance to see what the word "for" meant in this verse. It too was the word "eis," meaning "for," "unto," "toward," etc. Now here is where this gets very interesting and enlightening.

There is another "for" in Matthew 26:28 that comes before the phrase *"for the forgiveness of sins."* Let's take a look at the whole verse again to see what I'm talking about. *"Drink all of it, for this is My blood of the new testament, which is shed "**for**" many for the remission of sins."* (Matt. 26:28) Jesus states that His blood is being shed *"for many."* When I went to the Strong's Greek Concordance and looked up the word "for" in the phrase *"for many,"* guess what I found? The word "for" in the original Greek language that the text was written in is actually the word "peri."

You've probably already guessed what I found out next when I looked up the definition of "peri" in the Greek concordance. Yup, it means **"because of."** That's where the misunderstanding comes from. Of course, it makes perfect sense to use "peri" in the phrase *"for many,"* because Jesus is stating that He is going to die "because of" the many souls He is seeking to save. Unfortunately, for years people have been interpreting the word "for" in the phrase *"for the forgiveness of sins"* as the word "peri," meaning "because of" instead of the proper word "Eis" meaning "to" or "toward".

Wow! This was a huge revelation for me. I mean, this is the type of stuff that entire church denominations have been built upon. Why was God revealing it to a peon like me? Could it be simply because I was seeking the unadulterated truth about God and His church? Was it because my soul's desire was not to do my own will, but the pure will of our Divine Creator? Jesus did say that if we seek we will find. Was it really that easy? Is it all about having a pure heart and mind to seek and love God's truth with all of our heart, soul, mind, and strength?

I'm not sure I had the answer to all of those questions, but I did know one thing, if "for" were to be translated as "because of" in the phrase, *"for the remission of sins"* in Acts 2:38, it would be inconsistent with Acts 22:16, where Ananias told Paul to be *"baptized and wash away your sins."* Thus, being immersed in water was part of the "sin forgiving" process, according to Ananias.

Thinking back before Jesus died, all of Judea came to John The Baptizer confessing their sins in repentance and John immersed them in water *for the remission of sins* (John 1:29-34, 3:22-28, 4:1-2). This was the process that God had in place at that time for people to receive the forgiveness of their sins. This was a transition period between the old covenant and the new. Of course, their sins were rolled forward to when Jesus would die for them on the cross, just as our sins are rolled back to Christ's sacrifice on the cross.

Even Jesus consented to his disciples baptizing people under John's baptism for the forgiveness of their sins (John 1:24-34). There must be something very important about John's water baptism and it's foreshadowing of the forgiveness of sins under the New Covenant. But when I considered my baptism and its relation to the forgiveness of my sins, I became nervous because that's not why I was baptized. If I was totally honest with myself, my baptism was no more than a good thing to do and mimic what Jesus did when He was baptized by John. It didn't have anything to do with my salvation and the forgiveness of my sins.

I trembled at the thought of my soul being in jeopardy and dropped to my knees right then and there and prayed to God to show me the truth about "His" plan of salvation, and not my own. After further study in God's word, I learned that after the resurrection of Jesus, John's baptism was no longer valid, so those who knew only John's baptism were taught about the baptism into Christ and were re-baptized into Christ (Acts 18:24-28, Acts 19:1-6).

There it was, an example of folks being re-baptized after they had a better understanding. Was God trying to tell me something? Even if He was, I was resisting it tooth and nail. My pride would not let me believe that I might be wrong about something so important. I mean, my life had changed dramatically! How could that be if I'm not really a Christian? Or was I simply coming *"unto Christ,"* as Romans 10:10 states?

All throughout my studying, I kept my friend Greg up to date on what I was finding and feeling. He was very supportive and encouraged me to continue seeking the truth. Another passage I looked at was in Acts 16. A woman named Lydia was paying close attention to the preaching of Paul and she and her household were baptized. In the same chapter there was also a Philippian Jailer (Acts 16:25-34) who asked Paul and Silas, *"What must I do to be saved?"* They answered, *"Believe on the Lord Jesus Christ, and you and your household will be saved."*

Now wait a minute! There it is again! Another verse saying all you have to do is believe. Why does the Bible seem to be contradicting itself? There has to be an answer here somewhere. I continued to read over that passage again for clarification. Paul said that by believing on the Lord Jesus Christ, *"you and **your household** will be saved."* So I can believe in Jesus and the rest of my family will be saved? That doesn't sound right. But in the context of this passage, it made sense as I continued to read. The passage explains how Paul and Silas *"spoke the word of the Lord to him, **together with all who were in his house.**"* So when Paul was speaking to the Jailer, he was also preaching the gospel to those in his house. In response to the preaching of God's word, they all "believed" and were all baptized immediately (Acts 16:32-33). I took notice of the fact that they were all baptized immediately after they believed, unlike some baptismal ceremonies today that take place weeks or months after a person believes in Christ. This biblical account seemed to be consistent with many of the other verses I had studied recently, and with the urgency related to immersion in water being part of the sin-forgiving process.

With every verse I studied, I began to understand that if believing (or what some call "mental assent") is all that's needed to be saved, then what about the verse in James 2:19, which states, *"you believe there is one God, you do well, even the demons believe and tremble."* You and I know the demons aren't going to heaven, so is believing enough? These were some of the questions that were still swirling around in my finite head that needed eternal truth to iron out.

Speaking of demons, what about the one who confessed verbally that Jesus was the Christ, the Son of the living God (Mark 5:5-12)? Is that demon going to heaven too? And what about Repentance? Jesus said, *"unless you repent, you will all likewise perish" (Luke 13:3).* Peter also said Repent in Acts 2:38. So repentance is definitely necessary as well, right? Could water baptism be a prerequisite for being saved, born again, and forgiven of my sins, as a true Christian in the Lord's church?

I wanted to know if there were more verses that talked about baptism. So the next time I saw Greg at worship on Sunday, I asked him if he knew of more verses on baptism. And of course, he did. And was more than happy to share them with me. I say that sarcastically, but he was genuinely excited that I was so interested in studying about baptism. The additional verses he gave me were Galatians 3:26-27, Colossians 2:11-12, and 1 Peter 3:21. After worship was over, I couldn't wait to turn over to those verses and see what they had to say. Okay, to be honest, I peeked at a couple during worship, but don't tell anyone.

In verse 26 of Galatians chapter 3, Paul writes, *"for you are all sons of God through faith in Christ Jesus."* There it is again. We are sons of God *"through faith."* That's all it takes is faith and **"faith only"**. But let me continue to read and get more context. Verse 27 states, *"for as many of you as were baptized into Christ have put on Christ."* Oh no, there's that baptism again, and it looks like it's being included in the faith process of being *"in Christ."*

Now about this phrase *"into Christ"* in Galatians 3:27, the verses following verse 27 explained how we have to be *"In Christ"* to be heirs of His promise. So I wanted to know about being "in Christ," not just coming *"unto Christ,"* as Romans 10:9-10 states. I remember reading in Romans 6 where Paul said to the church in Rome that being baptized "into Christ" is a uniting of one's self with the death, burial, and resurrection of Christ. He wrote that Christians are *"buried with Him [Jesus] through baptism."* According to the Apostle Paul, the way we are united with Christ's death, for the forgiveness of our sins, is by being *"baptized into"* His death (Romans 6:1-5). It was beginning to sound like the difference between "into" and "unto" were pretty significant.

The next verse was Colossians 2:11-12. Paul is talking about the Christian undergoing a spiritual circumcision *"not made with hands,"* by *"putting off the sins of the flesh by the circumcision of Christ, buried with Him in baptism" (Col. 2:12).* This must be where the concept of baptism being a "type of circumcision" came from.

In the past I was not taught that the New Covenant water baptism of today was a "Uniting of oneself with Christ" and a *"burial with Him."* Nor was I taught that it was *"for the forgiveness of sins."* On the contrary, I was simply told that it was an "outward sign of an inward grace," something that had already taken place within me. Unfortunately, this teaching was not what I was finding in the Bible regarding the true function and purpose of baptism. In fact, I had yet to find the phrase "outward sign of an inward grace" anywhere in God's holy word.

"*Now Saves Us*"

This was amazing! I had no idea that all these previous verses on baptism existed in the New Testament. I had to admit that there were a lot of verses that supported the claim of water baptism being part of God's salvation process. But I still hadn't come across a verse that says "baptism will save me." Even today, I have read a lot of the Bible and have never read a verse stating that. Still, I wanted to be able to tell Greg that I read all the verses that he gave me on baptism and wanted to make sure I totally exhausted all that God had to say on the subject.

The last verse I read was 1 Peter 3:20-21. Peter was relating our salvation to that of Noah and the ark. He talked about how eight souls were *"saved through water."* Then in verse 21 of 1Peter, the Apostle Peter said that *"we have an antitype* (a like figure, or similar situation) *that **now saves us – baptism.***"

Have you ever had that feeling of shock that jump-starts your heart and sends what feels like an electric pulse throughout your body? I actually have had that feeling physically when I lived in Germany as a child. We had these converter boxes that transferred the electrical current from 220 volts (The European standard) to 110 volts (what we used in the U.S). Well, one day I was being careless while plugging in an extension cord, and got an electric shock as I accidentally touched part of the metal prong while plugging in the cord. My entire body was thrust back onto my bed, as if a professional wrestler had punched me in the chest and performed a body slam. It was absolutely amazing and terrifying at the same time. I'm just glad I'm still alive.

That's kind of how I felt when I read this verse. I had just read something that shook me to my core. I had just read something that I thought would never exist in the Bible. That terrified me. I could not accept the possibility of being wrong about my salvation all this time. My heart was beating like a kettledrum. All of the verses that I have read on baptism were summed up in this final verse in 1Peter 3:21.

I understood that Peter was explaining how - as the water aided Noah and his family in escaping the destruction taking place below them by being in the ark - we too have a similar situation where water also aides us in saving our souls from eternal destruction. If I understand Peter correctly, the like figure that we have today is the burial in water (baptism) that - preceded by belief in Jesus as the Christ, repentance of our sins, and confession of Jesus as the Son of God - brings us into Christ and washes away our sins (Acts 22:16). I could see it as clear as day now. Baptism was the burial that unites us with the death, burial, and resurrection of Jesus Christ almost 2000 years ago (Romans 6:1-5).

I had to read it again, because I still couldn't believe it. God said, *"we have an antitype* [similar situation] *"that now saves us – baptism."* Not simply getting wet and washing our outer body, but that baptism was an *"answer of a good conscience towards God" (1 Peter 3:21)*. Could it be true that if I were to **answer the gospel call of Jesus** in the true biblical way, I would believe in Jesus as the Son of God (John 3:16), repent of the sin I have committed (Luke 13:3), confess Jesus Christ as the risen Son of God (Matthew 10:32-33), and finally answer God's call in good conscience by being immersed in water for the forgiveness of my sins (Matthew 28:18, Acts 2:38, Acts 22:16, 1Peter 3:21)? And after doing so would God add me to His church, the body of Christ, **the church that Jesus built** (Matt. 16:18, Acts 2:47, Colossians 1:18)?

I realized that I had a decision to make. Was I going to stick with what I had learned and understood before thoroughly studying God's word? Or was I going to obey what the Bible was clearly teaching me? One thing I knew was that I didn't want to be a part of some man-made religious group that is based on the teachings and commandments of men.

I remembered Jesus saying, *"In vain they worship Me, teaching as doctrines the commandments of men" (Matt. 15:9)*. I wanted to be added to the one body (Ephesians 4:4-6) that was bought by the blood of Jesus Christ. I wanted to be in Christ's church, not John Calvin's church, or John Smyth's Church, or John Wesley's Church, or Martin Luther's church, or any generic non-denominational, evangelical church. I wanted to be in **the church that Jesus built**, the one that He is the head of (Col. 1:18), the church that He died for and is coming back to redeem. I wanted to know for a fact that what I did to become a Christian was exactly what God said to do under the New Covenant. And I wanted to have the book, chapter, and verse from the Bible for everything I believe and obey.

Yet, **for the life of me, I could not find the sinner's prayer in the Bible anywhere.** Although, I could find plenty of examples and commandments for people to believe, repent, confess and be immersed in water for the forgiveness of their sins, in order to be saved from eternal damnation.

The sweat on my hands began to dry up and the beating of my heart slowed down to a calm, consistent rhythm. I was beginning to let go of my own will and allow God's will to take over. He said He has given me "all" that I need *"pertaining to life and Godliness through the knowledge of Him"* (2Pet.1:1-3). And since God's word is the truth (John 17:17), I realized that I must abide in it, not in my emotions and preconceived notions, if I am going to be "set free" (John 8:31-32).

Yet, I still had one more question for God. Why did it seem like God was contradicting Himself or being inconsistent regarding His plan of salvation? Why was it that one verse in His word says to believe and another says to repent, then yet another says to confess and still another says to be baptized?

Summing It All Up

Wow! God is so good! He said if I seek the truth I would find it. And there it was, a verse that answered my question about all the different verses saying different things regarding the same subject. It was Psalm 119:160, which reads, *"The entirety (or sum) of thy word is truth."* So if we use mathematical terminology, as some translations do, we see that the *"**sum**"* of God's word is truth, meaning if we **"add up"** all the verses on a certain subject, we will get the "sum total" truth on the matter. Of course, we have to understand the dispensations and the fact that we are under the New Covenant today, not the Old Covenant, when adding up the verses on God's plan of salvation.

This helped me immensely in understanding why God did not have to put the total plan of salvation in every verse that speaks of salvation, but if we add up all the verses, we'll find the SUM to be the truth on the subject. Of course, for our salvation today, we would need to add up only those verses found in the New Testament, under the New Covenant, since Jesus nailed the Old Covenant to the cross (Colossians 2:14).

Therefore, I found that the whole truth on being born again, forgiven of my sins, saved from eternal damnation, and being added to the church that Jesus built, consists of: believing in Christ (John 3:16), repenting of my sin (Luke 13:3), confessing Jesus Christ as the risen Son of God (Romans 10:9-10), and being baptized (totally immersed in water) for the forgiveness of my sins (Mark 16:16, Matthew 28:18-19, Acts 2:38, Acts 8:38-39, Acts 10:48, Acts 16:32-33, Acts 22:16, Romans 6:1-5, Galatians 3:26-27, Ephesians 4:4, Colossians 2:12, 1 Peter 3:21).

But it doesn't stop there. No "Once saved, always saved" stuff. We have to continue to *"walk in the light"* and *"confess our sins"* so that the blood of Jesus can continue to cleanse us from all unrighteousness (1 John 1:7-9). If you ask me, God gives us plenty of commands and examples of how to become a true Christian today. We simply need to decide if we're going to do it God's way, as prescribed in the Bible, or rely on the traditions and practices of religious groups who seem to be following the *"commandments of men"* (Matt.15:9) instead of the inspired word of God.

"One Body"

The beautiful thing about Greg encouraging me to study the Bible is that he was not trying to push one church's teaching over another. He was simply trying to get me to read and study the Bible for myself. But I still wanted to look at the subject of the church and see what the inspired scriptures have to say about it. So I asked Greg and he gave me a few scriptures to investigate.

He began with a verse that I was familiar with, where Jesus says *"upon this rock I will build my church" (Matt. 16:18)*. One thing I noticed about this verse was that the word "church" was singular. And as I read the context of the passage, I learned that Jesus asked Peter, *"Who do you say that I am?"* and Peter replied, *"you are the Christ, the Son of the living God."* It was upon Peter's faithful response that **Jesus was the Christ**, that Jesus would build His church upon. Therefore, the building of God's church was not upon Peter himself, but upon what Peter said regarding Jesus being the Christ, the foundation and chief cornerstone of His church.

I continued to look up some other verses including the word "church" and found Colossians 1:18 which states *"He is the head of the body, the church."* The context of this verse was talking about Jesus and how He is the head of everything pertaining to His church. Yet, it was the phrase *"the body"* that I found to be very interesting. It stated that He, Jesus, was the head of *"the body."* Then it clarified that *"the body"* is also *"the church."*

Another verse that Greg suggested was Ephesians 4:3-5, where the Apostle Paul is discussing the unity that should exist in Christ's church. Paul wrote, *"There is one body and one Spirit, just as you were called in one hope of your calling; one Lord, one faith, one baptism".* As you might have figured out by now, the word **"one"** was beginning to stand out in my mind, as well as the word **"body."** First, Jesus said He would build *"His church,"* (singular). Then Paul said He, Jesus, is the head of ***"the body, the church,"*** (singular). Again in Ephesians 4:4 it states that there is *"one body."*

I wondered if there were more verses that referred to the church as "the body." So after a little more digging, I found Ephesians 5:23, which states that Christ is head of the church, and He is the *"Savior of the body."* If I was understanding this correctly, Jesus built His church on the faith that He is the Son of God (The Christ), that His church is also known as *"The Body,"* and that there is only *"one body"* of which Christ is *"the Savior."*

Again, if we keep in mind that *"the sum of His word is truth,"* and we use basic logic, it's pretty easy to conclude that Jesus established one church, or one body, that all people have to be baptized into, in order for Jesus to save them (*"we are baptized into one body,"* 1 Corin. 12:13) (*"He is the savior of the body,"* Eph. 5:23).

It's kind of like what Peter was talking about in 1 Peter 3:21, where all of those wanting to be saved from the flood had to be in the ark. During Noah's time there was only one ark to get into in order to be saved from the destruction. Likewise, today there is only one body of Christ to get into where salvation can be found.

Peter went on to say that we have something similar to the ark in these last days that *"now saves us – baptism."* And as Paul clarified, it is the baptism into Christ that unites us with His death, burial, and resurrection (Romans 6:3-5). Paul went on to clarify that there is only one proper baptism that put us into the one body of Christ, which is His church (Col. 1:18, Eph. 4:4).

As I continued to look at this word "body" and how it is used in connection with "the church," I looked again at Paul's analogy of the body, where he stated, *"we, being many, are one body in Christ, and individually members of one another" (1Cor. 12:12)*. And again, *"For as the body is one and has many members, but all the members of that one body, being many, are one body, so also is Christ." (1 Corinthians 12:20)*.

So if there is only one body, and the body is the church, the simple and logical deduction is that there is only one church that is actually the church that Jesus built. That church is also known as the Son's house (Hebrews 3:6). And as the old psalm says, *"unless the Lord build the house, they labor in vain that built it" (Psalm 127:1)*.

The Moment Of Truth

A huge burden was lifted from my heart. I no longer wondered if I did the right thing to become a Christian. I knew for a fact that I had not. I knew now that if I truly wanted to be forgiven of my sins and become a Christian in the church that Jesus is the Savior of, I needed to respond to the gospel in the way God taught me in the Bible.

Wow! What a decision to have to make. My own will was fighting me to the very end, but I knew that I had to be baptized for the forgiveness of my sins in order to be added to the true body of Christ (Acts 2:38), the one body of which Christ is the head (Acts 2:47, Eph. 4:1-4, Col. 1:18).

Early on in my spiritual walk, I had an incredible zeal for God, but it wasn't according to knowledge (Romans 10:2). I did not do what Jesus commanded me to do in order to have my sins forgiven. My belief in Jesus for salvation had brought me UNTO Christ, but I had not been reconciled to God by being united with the death of Jesus through a baptism for forgiveness. (Romans 6:1-5). I needed to be clothed with Christ if I was going to be added to His church (Gal. 3:27, Acts 2:47).

Still, in all my searching, I could not find one verse in the Bible that taught me to **pray my way into the body of Christ** or into a saved spiritual state. I now knew exactly what God wanted me to do in order for Him to wash away my sins and add me to His church. I had it in writing, straight from the Lord Himself. In 2 Thessalonians 1:8, God said He will bring *"vengeance on those who do not obey the gospel."* The Apostle Paul wrote *"I declare to you the gospel"* in 1 Corinthians 15:1, then went on to explain that the gospel was the death, burial and resurrection of Jesus Christ (1 Corinth. 15:1-4).

How then was one supposed to *obey* the death, burial, and resurrection of Jesus? Could it be by *"dying to one's self,"* being *"buried with Christ through baptism into death,"* and *"rising in newness of life,"* as stated in Romans 6: 1-7? Yes! And that's exactly what I wanted to do. But for some reason, I didn't go to the church congregation where Greg was attending to get baptized. I guess I was still a little too proud to submit to baptism where Greg was worshipping. Perhaps I was embarrassed that I had not known to do it earlier. So instead I returned to one of the "non-denominational" churches I had attended in the past and asked one of their ministers if I could be baptized. He hesitated for a second then said, "Sure, let me have one of our secretary's put you on the list for baptism." I thought to myself, "List?" Then gave into my suspicion and responded, "Great!" and started following him down the hall.

He led me to a side room, where he asked a woman to help me with my request. As we entered the room, he wished me well and left me in her care. "So you'd like to be baptized?" she asked. And I responded enthusiastically, "Yes!" "Okay, let's put you on our list." Then she pulled out a yellow legal pad from the desk and asked me for my name. I told her what it was, but was surprised that the pad she pulled out of the desk was blank. There wasn't even a heading of any sort on the pad. It was simply a blank pad of paper on which she wrote my name.

She went on to tell me that they conduct their baptisms once a year at another location and would be happy to accommodate me at that time. Of course, by this time I realized that I was in the wrong place. I guess I knew it all along, but needed one last confirmation. At that point I knew, if I was going to be baptized for the right reasons, at the right time, and in the right way, I needed to be with the right people who are teaching and practicing what the Bible teaches. I needed to be with the Lord's church who were "abiding in the Apostles doctrine" (Acts 2:42).

The next Sunday I attended the North East Philadelphia church of Christ, where Greg and his family were members. After the sermon, the preacher gave the call for those who wanted to become Christians by believing in Jesus, repenting of their sins, confessing Christ as the Son of God, and being baptized (immersed in water) for the forgiveness of their sins. After he was done, I went forward. Here I was again, answering another alter call. But this time it was different. This time I had book, chapter, and verse for what I was about to do. The preacher took my confession of faith in Christ, then took me to their pool of water behind the pulpit and immersed me in the name of The Father, The

Son, and the Holy Spirit for the forgiveness of my sins. He actually stated that he was baptizing me "for the forgiveness of sins". I knew right then and there that God, as He did with Paul in Acts 22:16, had washed my sins away. I was so excited that He also as stated in Acts 2:47, added me to His church!

This time around I was also crystal clear on the purpose for my submission to immersion in water. Now I knew why, months earlier, Greg asked me why I was baptized the first time. This time I could give him an answer straight out of the Bible. That was an awesome reality.

Needless to say, I rose "in newness of life." My friend Greg's eyes were glazed over with tears of joy. Not only for my decision to obey the gospel, but also for his older brother who had decided to obey the gospel that same morning as well. And like the Ethiopian Eunuch, "we both went on our way rejoicing!"

As I continued to grow as a Christian, I learned that I was being redundant by calling myself a "Born-Again Christian" earlier in my quest for truth. A Christian is assumed to be "Born Again" by what Jesus taught Nicodemus in the Gospel of John, chapter 3. So as far as what I should call myself, I noticed in Acts 11:26 the followers of Christ were called *"Christians first in Antioch."* And in 1 Peter 4:16 it states, *"if anyone suffers **as a Christian**, let him glorify God **in this name**" (ESV).* So if I'm going to call myself anything, it's going to be a "Christian," and a Christian only.

Still, there was one thing that really concerned me a great deal. It was the millions of sincere and dedicated people in the world today who consider themselves to be Christians, yet have not obeyed the Gospel in the manner in which Jesus and His Apostles prescribed in the Bible. This is the reason why I wrote this book. Those people are basically in the same boat that I was in. It is my prayer that millions of believers in Christ will be encouraged to study the scriptures with an open heart, seeking out the truth regarding the salvation process that God has clearly provided us in His holy word, the Bible.

God has made his plan and process extremely simple to understand. Unfortunately, God has an adversary who will do what he can to confuse the minds of mankind. Remember how he deceived Eve by simply adding one little word to God's command, by saying that she would *"not" surely die* if she disobeyed God? Well, the enemy hasn't changed much over the years. If he can get man to add or take away a little of God's word and believe it, he can deceive us and have us thinking we're saved, when what we've obeyed was the teachings and commandments of men (Matt. 15:9), instead of the pure, unadulterated Word of God.

One Thing To Consider

While I was learning all this stuff from God's word, I felt compelled to bounce it off of people that I respected spiritually, like the "Pastor" at the church I was attending or a family member or friend whose spiritual opinion I respected. As I presented the scriptures I was studying, they gave me their take on them, which was the same thing I had been taught regarding those scriptures before I had actually read them and studied them myself. I soon realized that I could find someone to agree with me on any Bible subject almost anywhere. This was simply because they were under the same false teaching I was under. Many of them found it hard to see the scriptures at face value, but instead interpreted them through a Calvinistic or Evangelical viewpoint.

You may be thinking of consulting your "Pastor," family members, or friends as well. If you do, let me encourage you to stick with what the Bible teaches, and encourage them to do so, as well.

The most difficult part of realizing that you may not have obeyed the gospel the way God wants you to is the harsh reality of those who are in the same boat as you. Depending on who you know, this could mean hundreds of people including close family members, such as your mother, father, or grandparents. The focus at this point needs to be your own soul's salvation and making sure you are "in Christ" and have obeyed the gospel as prescribed in The New Testament. Remember, Jesus said, *"narrow is the gate, and difficult the way that leads to righteousness, and **few** there are that find it"* (Matthew 7:14).

Several years after I obeyed the gospel, the preacher of the church I was attending and I were having a personal bible study with a young couple. After sharing some of the same verses I mentioned earlier in this book, the husband's eyes began to well up with tears, and he said to us, "If what I'm reading is true, then all the people I know, who consider themselves to be Christians, are not saved. Because none of them have done what this is saying to do, and don't understand what I'm beginning to understand." We simply encouraged him to be honest and obedient to the scriptures, and then do his best to get others to see what he is beginning to see. Long story short, he and his wife were baptized into Christ for the forgiveness of their sins, and are still faithful members of Christ's church today.

It is always our hope that others will see the truth and obey it as well. But keep in mind that, in the judgment, we will all stand before God individually and give an account of our own individual decisions.

I hope you will prove God's word to be true by earnestly studying the New Testament. Jesus said, *"seek and you will find."* So if you seek out the truth with all of your heart, mind, soul, and strength, you will definitely find it!

I encourage you to be a seeker of truth, not the traditions and "commandments of men" (Matt 15:9).

More Characteristics Of The Lord's Church

With all the Christian-based churches in the world today, one might ask, "How can I know for sure which church is the one Jesus built?" To answer this question, God gives us an analogy in 1 Corinthians 12:12-26. As with our physical bodies, God's spiritual body (the church) has certain physical characteristics that will allow us to identify it when we see it.

Paul talks about our physical bodies having specific characteristics, like hands, eyes, and feet. He then explains that the same is true for God's spiritual body (the church). Therefore, if I wanted to find the church that Jesus built in the world today, I can observe what a church is teaching and practicing, and compare it with the characteristics of the church in the Bible. This was a comforting discovery, to know that I could identify the Lord's church in the world today by comparing it to the church in the New Testament. Of course, it meant that I needed to know my Bible pretty well to make the assessment.

After learning how to obey the gospel, I did my best to attend Wednesday night Bible study and worship on Sunday mornings and evenings at the Northeast Philadelphia church of Christ. Greg and my new brothers and sisters in Christ continued to help teach me some of the basic characteristics of the Lord's church. One of the first characteristics that they helped me understand had to do with the type of music found present in the church that Jesus built.

The Sacrifice Of Praise

One of the questions I had regarding the church of Christ's worship service had to do with the absence of instrumental music. Remember when I told Greg that they were "dead"? One of the reasons I said that pertained to the absence of instruments of music being played during their worship service. "So where is the piano or organ?" I asked one of my new brothers in Christ one Sunday morning. He was quick to encourage me to research the use of musical instruments, in reference to spiritual music and worship, in the New Testament. I was totally ready for this study and was excited to let Greg know that I was on another quest for truth about music in the Lord's church. I told him that I remembered reading somewhere that David used instruments to praise God. So I began my search with verses like 2 Samuel 6:2 and Psalm 150:4.

These verses clearly stated that instruments were used in praise to God by the nation of Israel. It was in the Bible, so why not use them today? But then came a question from Greg, as I shared these verses with him, that had me puffing my cheeks out again and saying, "What you talkin' about, Willis?" as he asked, "What about the New Covenant?" "I think I know where you're going," I replied. He continued, "Is there any mention of an instrument being used in worship or praise to God under the

New Covenant, after the death of Jesus, or in the entire New Testament?"

I thought for a second and said, "I don't know." Sure enough, when I went back and used every concordance and reference I could find, there was no mention of an instrument being used by Jesus, the Apostles, nor anyone else on earth, in praise or worship to God in the New Testament. This was another one of those "Aah Haah!" moments when I sat back in my chair, shaking my head and wondering how can this be?

I had experienced many types of churches and all of them had some type of musical instrument as part of their worship service. Yet in all of the New Testament, and under the New Covenant, there is no mention of anyone worshiping God with a musical instrument? What did this all mean? Why are so many churches taking part in this practice when there is no authority from God to do it in this current Christian dispensation? You thought I was puzzled about baptism? This one really threw me for a loop.

Through my study of the covenants, the Old Covenant versus the New Covenant, I was led to Hebrews chapters 8, 9, and 10. These chapters explained to me clearly that we, who are in Christ today, are under a *"better covenant, with better promises" (Hebrews 8:6).* The Old Covenant has been **"done away with"** having become **"obsolete"** (Heb. 8:13), while Hebrews 9:15 states that Christ *"is the Mediator of the **new covenant.**"*

The blood of bulls and goats was no longer a valid sacrificial system, nor were the grain offerings and system of worship under the law of Moses. The first verse in Hebrews chapter one states that, *"God, who in various times and various ways spoke to the fathers by the prophets (Moses, etc.), has in these last days spoken to us by His Son (Jesus Christ)"*. Therefore, it is the teaching of Jesus and His Apostles that we must adhere to today. To emphasize the contrast between the old law and the new covenant in Christ, John wrote, *"the law came by Moses, but grace and truth came by Jesus Christ"* (John 1:17).

In Colossians, it also states that God had taken the *"handwriting of ordinances* (the Old Testament Law) *that was against us, and nailed it to the cross"* (Col. 2:14). This was evidenced in Acts 2:42, where it records that the early church *"continued in the Apostles teaching,"* not in the teaching of Moses.

Realizing that the Old Testament pattern of worship and praise to God was no longer valid, I had to find out what Jesus and the Apostles authorized under the New Covenant. Thus, I sought out verses in the New Testament pertaining to any kind of music in reference to God. Much to my surprise, all I could find were the following verses: Ephesians 5:19, Colossians 3:16, James 5:13, and Hebrews 13:15-16. They all had one thing in common - when it came to the type of music God wanted from Christians in His church, God said, *"sing."* Even when Jesus was still alive, the only type of music He offered the Father was that He and the disciples *"sung a hymn"* (Matt. 26:30).

Talk about seeing someone's eyes pop wide open and jaw drop to the floor – again! This was crazy! How could I have not noticed that there were no commands, examples, or even suggestions of an instrument being played in worship to God in the New Testament? More importantly, how could millions of people, who profess to be Christians, not have noticed it? Why are they worshipping God with instruments, when God never authorized it under the New Covenant?

Jesus stated that it's by His word that we will be judged (John 12:48). So if people who consider themselves to be Christians, rightly dividing the word of truth (2 Timothy 2:15), and understanding the differences between worship under the Old Covenant and the New Covenant, why would they include mechanical instruments in their worship to God when there is no authority given by Jesus or the Holy Spirit in the New Testament?

Needless to say, this was a very difficult thing for me to swallow. I tried every avenue, every hypothetical situation, every rationalization to discount the whole instrumental music subject. I tried statements like, **"but God's word doesn't say we can't do it."** This was a basic mistake in logic on my part. It was obvious to me, although I didn't want to admit it, that God did not have to put all the things that He did "not" want us to do in the Bible, but rather only those things that we must do, or that He does authorize.

For instance, when we observe the Lord's Supper, the example is to use *"Unleavened Bread"* and the *"Fruit of the vine"* (Luke 22:1-20, Acts 20:7) Since God chose to include these types of foods for the Lord's Supper in His word, it clearly eliminates all other types. He did not have to include the hundreds of foods that He "does not" want us to use for the Lord's Supper, but only those two that He authorized.

So using my brain and the logic that God gave me, I realized that the same logic had to be used for the subject of music in worship to God. If God clearly states in His Word for Christians to *"Sing and make melody in their hearts" (Ephesians 5:19, Colossians 3:16)*, then it's obvious to me now that He did not have to include all the instruments He did not want me to use. He simply authorized one instrument that all Christians must use in praising His Name, by singing from the heart. He even told us in Hebrews 13:15-16 that when it comes to offering a sacrifice of praise, He is *"well pleased"* with the *"fruit of our lips."*

Now, if you're like me, you really like instrumental music in your worship service. Yet, that brings up a good question. Who's worship service is it, yours or God's? If I wanted to stick to my guns, as far as doing things God's way and not my own, I had to accept what the Bible was teaching me, even though it wasn't making a whole lot of sense at the moment, because they used instruments under the Old Covenant, and there will supposedly be some in heaven, so why not now? Still, I had to trust God more than my own understanding (Proverbs 3:5). I realized that if I wanted to be pleasing to God, then the music I offer to God would have to be according to what pleases Him and what He authorized me to do under the New Covenant.

Wow! I was finally beginning to understand why the true church that Jesus built only sings acapella music in their worship service. It was one of the more easily recognizable characteristics of the Lord's body in today's day and age. And with all that Jesus instructed the Apostles to continue to teach His followers, instrumental accompaniment in music offered to God was not one of them. I was still amazed that in all of His inspired instructions throughout the New Testament, the only authorized form of music, in worship and praise to God, under the Christian dispensation, is singing. That was pretty amazing to me (Eph. 5:19).

I couldn't wait to get back to Bible study the next Wednesday night and share with Greg and the brother I had spoken with what I had found regarding instruments of praise in the Lord's church. They were elated and were encouraged by my willingness to seek the truth on the matter and not simply go with what I thought was right without having studied the scriptures. I kept going back in my mind to when Jesus said, *"Seek and you will find."* As I continued to seek, I continued to grow ever cognizant of the truth in His statement.

The Lord's Supper

While worshiping with my fellow brothers and sisters in Christ at the Northeast Philadelphia church of Christ, another characteristic of the church that Jesus built was evident every Sunday as we observed the Lord's Supper.

Having experienced several types of so-called Christian churches before obeying the gospel, I witnessed various practices when it came to taking communion. Some did it once a month, others only during special days throughout the year. In keeping with the commands and examples we read in the New Testament, when it came to the Lord's church observing the communion, it was observed every first day of the week.

Jesus began by commanding the Apostles to take the *"bread which is my body"* and the *"cup of the new testament in My blood"* in remembrance of Him (Matthew 26:26–28; Mark 14:22–24, Luke 22:19–20). After the church of Christ began in Acts chapter 2, we read of them partaking of the Lord's supper in Acts 20:7, where it states that *"upon the first day of the week, when the disciples came together to break bread, Paul preached unto them, ready to depart on the morrow,"* Now, how do we know that "the breaking of bread" is referring to the Lord's Supper and not just an ordinary meal that they were sharing? The Apostle Paul gives us more understanding as he writes, *"The cup of blessing which we bless, is it not the communion of the blood of Christ?* **The bread which we break**, *is it not the communion of the body of Christ?"* (1 Corinthians 10:16). Paul gives Christians additional inspired instructions regarding the Lord's Supper in 1 Corinthians 11, beginning with verse 17. Unfortunately, in this instance the church was not partaking of the communion correctly, so Paul had to admonish them by writing, *"Now in giving these instructions I do not praise you, since you* **come together** *not for the better but for the worse. For first of all, when you* **come together as a church**, *I hear that there are divisions among you, and in part I believe it. For there must also be factions among you, that those who are approved may be recognized among you. Therefore when you* **come together in one place**, *it is* **not** *to eat the* **Lord's Supper**. *For in eating, each one takes his* **own supper** *ahead of others; and one is hungry and another is drunk. What! Do you not have* **houses to eat and drink in?** *Or do you despise the church of God and shame those who have nothing? What shall I say to you? Shall I praise you in this? I do not praise you."*

Notice how the Apostle Paul starts out by clarifying that this is a special occasion when the members of the Lord's body ***"come together as a church."*** This is in keeping with Acts 20:7 which states that *"upon the first day of the week, the disciples* **came together to break bread."** Although they were supposed to be coming together to partake of the Lord's Supper, this group of

Christians in Corinth were treating this *"breaking of bread"* as their **"own supper."** To which Paul rebukes them by saying, *"Do you not have houses to eat and drink in?"* This is to say, when you come together as the Lord's church to break bread, this is not a common meal that you would eat and drink at home. This is the "Lord's Supper" not your "own supper" and should be observed and conducted in the proper manner. Paul goes on to give them further instructions on how to properly partake of the communion in 1 Corinthians 11:23:

"For I received from the Lord that which I also delivered to you: that the Lord Jesus on the same night in which He was betrayed took bread; and when He had given thanks, He broke it and said, Take, eat; this is My body which is broken for you; do this in remembrance of Me. In the same manner He also took the cup after supper, saying, This cup is **the new covenant** *in My blood. This do, as often as you drink it, in remembrance of Me. For* **as often as you eat this bread and drink this cup,** *you proclaim the Lord's death till He comes."*

How often did they break the bread and drink the cup of communion with the Lord together "as a church"? Acts 20:7 informs us that it was on the *"first day of the week."* Therefore, from the previous passages, we learn that the first century church of Christ "came together as a church" on the "first day of the week" to "break bread." This breaking of bread was a "communion with the body of Christ," also known as the "Lord's Supper."

Jesus himself instructed His disciples to partake of the Supper in remembrance of Him. Thus, if we are to emulate the characteristics and practices of the Lord's church regarding the Lord's Supper, we will partake of it *"on the first day of the week."* If we think of this logically, we understand that "the first day of the week" takes place every week. Therefore, we have no other course but to conclude that the first century church observed the Lord's Supper every Sunday.

This is one of many examples where God requires us to use our own logic and deductive reasoning to understand His will for our lives. Still, someone may say, "But the Bible doesn't specifically state that we have to take the Lord's Supper every week." This is where an **example** of what the first century church did is as good as a **direct command.** God placed in His inspired word an example of when the Lord's church observed the communion. By God clarifying "the first day of the week," He excluded all other days, and at the same time specified the "first day." The same logic must be used when it comes to the emblems of food that are used during the Lord's Supper. Bread and the fruit of the vine is what Jesus used when instituting the Lord's Supper. Jesus doesn't have to name all the other foods that we should not use. By His example of using bread and grape juice, it excludes all other foods.

As mentioned earlier, this same logic is used in understanding how mechanical instruments of music, in worship to God, are not authorized by

Him under the New Testament. God in His inspired word specified "singing" as the form of music that He desires from His children, under the New Covenant. The same goes for how often Christians should observe the Lord's Supper and what foods to use.

Pastors

Another characteristic of the church that Jesus built is its understanding of the word "Pastor." Who do you think of when you hear the word "Pastor"? Is it the main preacher or minister of a church? That's what I thought. It's also usually the answer from most people who call themselves Christian. Although, those who are members of the "Lord's" church understand that it's not the preacher, but the Elders, Shepherds, and Overseers of the congregation. And there are always more than one.

Knowing how a verse reads in the original language (Greek, when it pertains to the New Testament) is very important in understanding its meaning. Studying the Greek translation of the word "Pastor" I found that it's from the Greek word "Poimen," which is defined as "Shepherd" or "Elder" also known as "the Overseers of Christian Assemblies." In Acts 20:17 it states that the Apostle Paul called for the ***"Elders"*** of the church of Ephesus to come to him. When they did, he said to them in verse 28 of Acts 17, *"Therefore take heed to yourselves and to all the flock, among which the Holy Spirit has made you **overseers**, to **shepherd** the church of God which He purchased with His own blood."*

Therefore, if a Pastor is a Shepherd, and a Shepherd is an Overseer, and an Overseer is an Elder, then the Pastor is not the main preacher of a congregation. The Pastors occupy a different position and role than the Senior Minister of a church congregation. The Pastors are those who shepherd the church and oversee all of its teaching, services, benevolence, funds, and even the Senior Minister himself. This truth is in stark contrast to what we see taking place in various so-called "Christian" churches throughout the world, where the Preacher or Senior Minister is the leader and head of the church. This structure does not exist in the church that Jesus built.

The Apostle Peter also instructed the **Elders** of the church to *"Shepherd the flock of God which is among you, serving as **overseers**" (1Peter 5:2).* Notice how all the verses that pertain to the Pastors or Elders of a church congregation in the New Testament are always plural. This of course implies that there must be more than one. When Paul instructed Titus to lead the congregation in appointing Elders, he wrote, *"set in order the things that are lacking, and appoint **Elders** (plural) in every city" (Titus 1:5).*

To compound this truth, the word "Pastor" (singular) does not exist in the New Testament (the portion of scripture where we find instruction for the church, under the New Covenant). When the scriptures speak of this specific position within the Lord's church, it's always referred to in the plural sense, as "pastors." Of course, biblical pastors (those who are elders according to the scriptures) can also preach from the pulpit, but the New Testament does not speak of a singular preacher being the pastor of the Lord's church and overseeing and shepherding the congregation. There is also no prerequisite for biblical pastors to preach the word, although they must be able to teach.

So can anybody be a Pastor? Not according to the inspired word of God. Continuing in Titus 1, verse 6, the Apostle Paul clarifies the qualities that Pastors (Elders) must have, writing, *"If a man is blameless, the husband of one wife, having faithful children..."* In this verse we see several requirements for the Elder, one being that he is a man. Secondly, he must be married. Thirdly, he must have children.

"Why would God require this?" was one of my first thoughts when I first read this, but as my studies continued, I found God's answer in 1 Timothy 3:5. Paul is instructing Timothy on the position of Elders in the Lord's church and writes by inspiration, *"For if a man does not know how to rule his own house, how will he take care of the church of God?"*

Thus, a Pastor in the church that Jesus built must be a godly husband and loving father to his children, and rule his own house well. This is required in order for him to be considered as one of the Pastors of a congregation of Christ's church.

Consider what Paul wrote to Timothy regarding Pastors (Shepherds, Elders, Overseers):

"This is a faithful saying: If a man desires the position of an Overseer (some translations say Bishop or Elder), *he desires a good work. 2. A bishop then must be blameless, the husband of one*

wife, temperate, sober-minded, of good behavior, hospitable, able to teach; not given to wine, not violent, not greedy for money, but gentle, not quarrelsome, not covetous; one who rules his own house well, having his children in submission with all reverence (for if a man does not know how to rule his own house, how will he take care of the church of God?); not a novice, lest being puffed up with pride he fall into the same condemnation as the devil. Moreover he must have a good testimony among those who are outside, lest he fall into reproach and the snare of the devil."

As we can read clearly in God's word, the work of the Pastors is much more than preaching from the pulpit. As a matter of fact, in all the prerequisites in the verses above, preaching is never mentioned. This is why it's important to know the identity of the church that Jesus built and the biblical definition of Pastors.

In Conclusion

Two years after being baptized into Christ, I met a beautiful Christian woman at a Wednesday Night Bible Study. That's why I tell young people to go to Wednesday Night Bible Study. Aside from the spiritual nourishment and fellowship, you never know what the Lord may have waiting for you!

She had obeyed the gospel the same way I did when she was sixteen years old. But now, she was twenty-four and I was twenty-eight. After dating for a year, I knew I wanted to spend the rest of my life as her husband, so I asked her to marry me. And she said, "Yes!" We were engaged for 9 months before tying the knot. The year we got married was a whirlwind. I got laid off from my job, we had a death in the family, and we moved to Connecticut when I was hired by the world's largest sports broadcasting network (ESPN) to design still and motion graphics for television.

A year later our first son was born. After three more years, God blessed us with another son. Our spiritual home became the South Road church of Christ in Farmington, CT. At this point, I was living an abundant life that only Jesus could have given me. Of course I knew that I was not worthy of it, and that it was by the grace of God and obedience to His will, that I was able to be the husband, father, Elder in His church, employee, and man that I am now. For this, I owe God all the honor, glory, and praise!

My wife Leila is now a cancer survivor and advocate for natural medicine, having developed and been a guest speaker at several Wellness Events for woman of the church of Christ. Learn more about her story at leilawashington.com

Finally, my friend, Jesus said, *"If you abide in my word, you are my disciples indeed, and you will know the truth and the truth will set you free"* (John 8:31-32).

I pray that you will seek out the truth of God in His Word - the Bible - and obey the gospel. For the most part, you can find people preaching and practicing what the Bible teaches at congregations of the churches of Christ throughout the world. But be sure to check what they teach and practice, to make sure you are among those whom God has added to His church, the church that Jesus built.

For a directory of congregations of the Lord's church, go to www.21stcc.com

For a free bible study course, go to:
https://www.worldbibleschool.org

Tommie Lee Washington III
Website: tommieleewashington.com

Made in the USA
Columbia, SC
30 October 2024